D0531802

EXPLORING SPACE

Pluto

by Colleen Sexton

Consultant:
Duane Quam, M.S. Physics
Chair, Minnesota State
Academic Science Standards
Writing Committee

BLASTOFF! READERS

BELLWETHER MEDIA · MINNEAPOLIS, MN

Note to Librarians, Teachers, and Parents:

Blastoff! Readers are carefully developed by literacy experts and combine standards-based content with developmentally appropriate text.

Level 1 provides the most support through repetition of high-frequency words, light text, predictable sentence patterns, and strong visual support.

Level 2 offers early readers a bit more challenge through varied simple sentences, increased text load, and less repetition of high-frequency words.

Level 3 advances early-fluent readers toward fluency through increased text and concept load, less reliance on visuals, longer sentences, and more literary language.

Level 4 builds reading stamina by providing more text per page, increased use of punctuation, greater variation in sentence patterns, and increasingly challenging vocabulary.

Level 5 encourages children to move from "learning to read" to "reading to learn" by providing even more text, varied writing styles, and less familiar topics.

Whichever book is right for your reader, Blastoff! Readers are the perfect books to build confidence and encourage a love of reading that will last a lifetime!

This edition first published in 2010 by Bellwether Media, Inc.

No part of this publication may be reproduced in whole or in part without written permission of the publisher. For information regarding permission, write to Bellwether Media, Inc., Attention: Permissions Department, 5357 Penn Avenue South, Minneapolis, MN 55419.

Library of Congress Cataloging-in-Publication Data

Sexton, Colleen A., 1967-
  Pluto / by Colleen Sexton.
    p. cm. – (Blastoff! Readers. Exploring space)
  Includes bibliographical references and index.
  Summary: "Introductory text and full-color images explore the physical characteristics and discovery of the dwarf planet Pluto. Intended for students in kindergarten through third grade"–Provided by publisher.
  ISBN 978-1-60014-410-3 (hardcover : alk. paper)
  1. Pluto (Dwarf planet)–Juvenile literature. I. Title.
  QB701.S49 2010
  523.49'22–dc22   2009038025

Text copyright © 2010 by Bellwether Media, Inc.
Printed in the United States of America, North Mankato, MN.

010110   1149

Contents

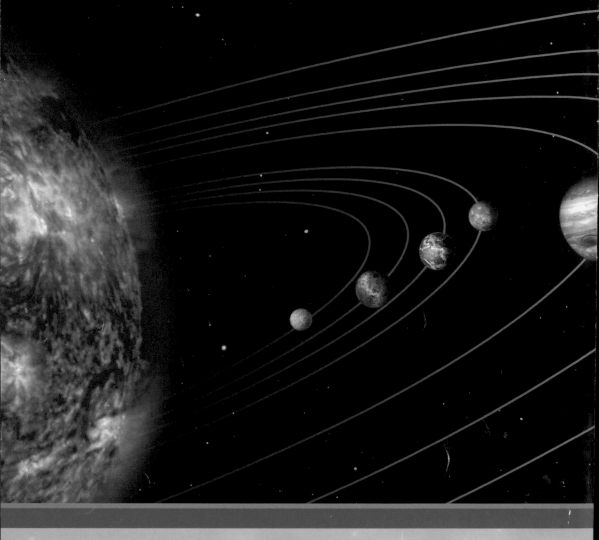

Pluto was discovered in 1930.
For 76 years, it was the ninth **planet**
in the **solar system**.

Pluto

In 2006, **astronomers** decided that Pluto did not meet new rules for being a planet. Pluto became a **dwarf planet**.

Dwarf planets are round.
They **orbit** the sun just
like planets do.

Unlike planets, dwarf planets share their orbits with other space objects.

Pluto is in the **Kuiper Belt** with thousands of other space objects. Kuiper Belt objects orbit the sun in a wide ring at the edge of the solar system.

Kuiper Belt

Pluto is farther from the sun than any planet. The sun is about 3.7 billion miles (5.9 billion kilometers) away from Pluto.

Pluto's orbit is different
from the orbits of the planets.
It makes a long, oval path
around the sun.

Pluto sometimes travels closer to the sun than Neptune. Neptune is the farthest planet from the sun.

Neptune

Pluto

A year on Pluto equals about 248 Earth years. That is how long it takes Pluto to travel once around the sun.

A day on Pluto equals about six Earth days. That is how long it takes Pluto to spin once on its **axis**.

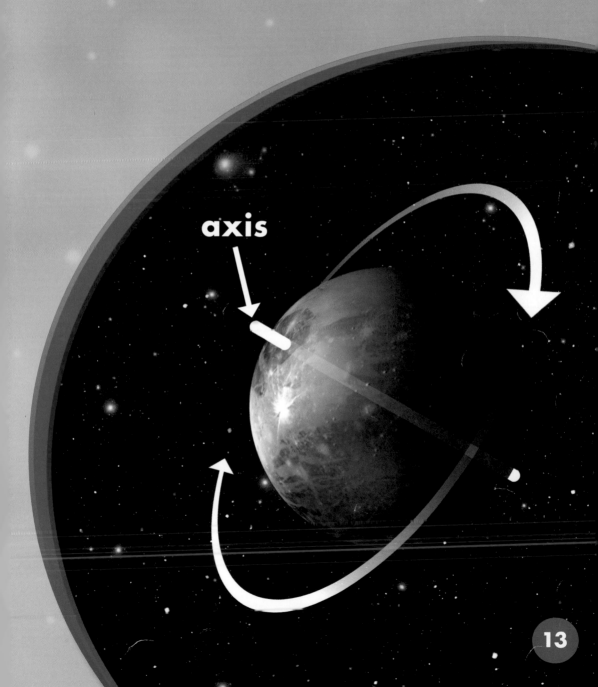

axis

Pluto is a small, light brown ball of rock and ice. It is 1,422 miles (2,288 kilometers) wide.

Some of the ice turns to gas when Pluto travels close to the sun. The gas forms an **atmosphere** around Pluto.

The sun looks like a bright **star** in Pluto's dark sky. Its light takes about five hours to reach Pluto.

Pluto is cold. It gets little of the sun's heat. The surface temperature is about -385° Fahrenheit (-232° Celsius).

Pluto

Charon

Pluto has three known **moons**. The largest moon is Charon. It is just over half the size of Pluto.

Two small moons also orbit Pluto. Hydra and Nix are each less than 40 miles (64 kilometers) wide.

Nix

Hydra

Scientists cannot see Pluto clearly, even with the strongest **telescopes**. It is too far away.

telescope

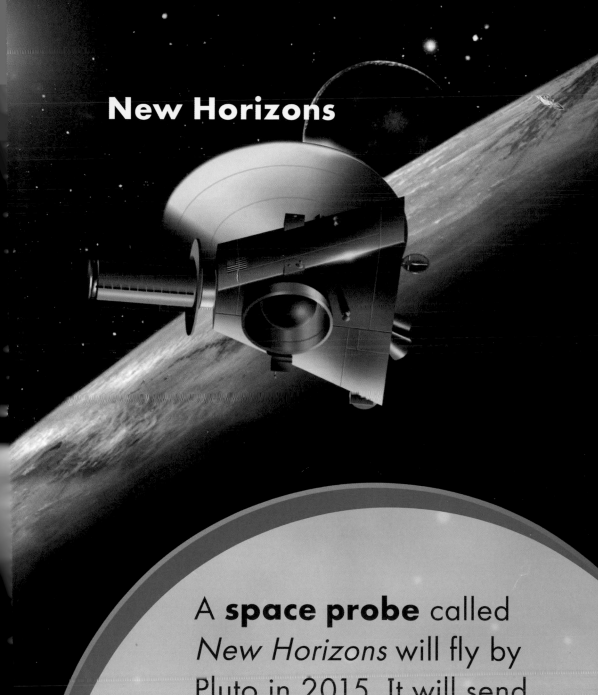

New Horizons

A **space probe** called *New Horizons* will fly by Pluto in 2015. It will send the first close-up pictures of Pluto back to Earth!

Glossary

astronomers—scientists who study space and objects in space

atmosphere—the gases around an object in space

axis—an imaginary line that runs through the center of a planet; a planet spins on its axis.

dwarf planet—a round space object that is not a moon and orbits the sun; dwarf planets share their orbits with other large space objects.

Kuiper Belt—a large area in the outer part of the solar system that has thousands of small space objects

moons—space objects that orbit a planet or other space object

orbit—to travel around the sun or other object in space

planet—a large, round space object that orbits the sun and is alone in its orbit

solar system—the sun and the objects that orbit it; the solar system has planets, moons, comets, and asteroids.

space probe—a spacecraft that explores planets and other space objects and sends information back to Earth; space probes do not carry people.

star—a large ball of burning gases in space; the sun is a star.

telescopes—tools that make faraway objects look larger and nearer; large telescopes can see deep into space.

To Learn More

AT THE LIBRARY

Kudlinski, Kathleen V. *Boy, Were We Wrong about the Solar System*. New York, N.Y.: Dutton Children's Books, 2008.

Rusch, Elizabeth. *The Planet Hunter: The Story Behind What Happened to Pluto*. Flagstaff, Ariz.: Rising Moon, 2007.

Wimmer, Teresa. *Pluto*. Mankato, Minn.: Creative Education, 2008.

ON THE WEB

Learning more about Pluto is as easy as 1, 2, 3.

1. Go to www.factsurfer.com.

2. Enter "Pluto" into the search box.

3. Click the "Surf" button and you will see a list of related Web sites.

With factsurfer.com, finding more information is just a click away.

BLASTOFF! JIMMY CHALLENGE

Blastoff! Jimmy is hidden somewhere in this book. Can you find him? If you need help, you can find a hint at the bottom of page 24.

Index

The images in this book are reproduced through the courtesy of: Byron W. Moore, front cover, p. 13; NASA, pp. 4-5, 8-9, 19 (small), 20-21; Detlev van Ravensway / Photo Researchers Inc., pp. 6-7; Juan Martinez, p. 9 (small); Juan Eppardo, pp. 10-11, 12; Diego Barucco, pp. 14-15; John Foster / Science Photo Library, p. 15 (small); Chris Butler / Science Photo Library, pp. 16-17, 18-19.

Blastoff! Jimmy Challenge (from page 23).
Hint: Go to page 21 and look to the "horizon."